The Hare and the Tortoise

Oxford University Press, Walton Street, Oxford OX2 6DP

OXFORD NEW YORK TORONTO
DELHI BOMBAY CALCUTTA MADRAS KARACHI
KUALA LUMPUR SINGAPORE HONG KONG TOKYO
NAIROBI DAR ES SALAAM CAPE TOWN
MELBOURNE AUCKLAND MADRID

and associated companies in
BERLIN IBADAN

Oxford is a trade mark of Oxford University Press

Hardback ISBN 0 19 279625 9 Paperback ISBN 0 19 272126 7

© Brian Wildsmith 1966, First published 1966.
Reprinted 1968, 1969, 1971, 1973, 1974, 1982 (twice), 1984, 1985, 1987, 1988, 1989, 1990, 1991, 1992, 1993

Paperback edition first published 1982.
Reprinted 1983, 1984, 1985, 1986, 1987, 1988, 1989, 1990, 1991, 1992

Printed in Hong Kong

Based on the fable by La Fontaine

BRIAN WILDSMITH

The Hare and
the Tortoise

OXFORD UNIVERSITY PRESS

A hare and a tortoise were having an argument. The hare, who could run very fast, thought he was much

more clever than the tortoise, who could only move slowly and had to carry his house around on his back.

But the tortoise did not agree. To the hare's surprise the tortoise challenged him to a race. "We will run from here, over the hill, through the hedge, then along the carrot field to the old cart," he said. The hare laughed. "I am sure to win, but we will race if you like."

News of the race spread quickly, and the birds and animals gathered to watch.

"The tortoise will not have a chance!" cried the fox.
"Wait and see," said the owl.

The cock offered to start the race. The spectators
stood back, and the cock swelled up ready to give
the signal.

"Cock-a-doodle-doo!" In a flash the hare was off, flying over the grass. The tortoise had hardly moved.

In a few moments
the hare had run
over the hill and
reached the hedge.
He looked behind, but
the tortoise was not
in sight. The hare
stopped to nibble
some tasty leaves.

The tortoise plodded on, and came to the hill. It was hard work for him to climb it, and the birds called

encouragement to help him on his way.

The hare had finished eating the leaves in the hedge and dashed off again at full speed to the carrot field. He was very fond of carrots and could not resist stopping to eat some.

He ate and ate until he was
so full he had to lie down and sleep
for a while.

The tortoise had only just reached the hedge.

He was already tired, but kept walking slowly on.

At last he reached the carrot field, but the hare
was too fast asleep to notice him passing by.

Suddenly the hare woke up. He stared in astonishment towards the old cart, the winning post. The tortoise was almost there!

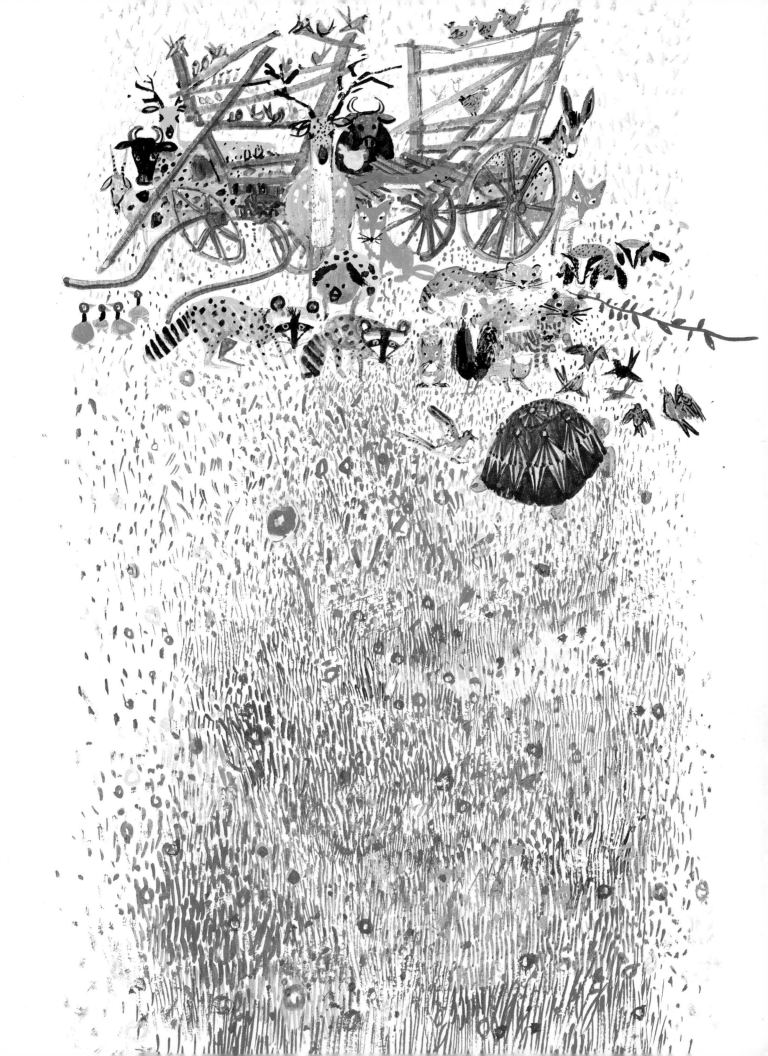

The hare ran as fast as he could but it was no use —the tortoise had won the race!

All the animals gathered round the tortoise while
he told how, in his slow and steady way, he had
won the race from the quick and careless hare.